OHIO STATE BUCKEYES

DEREK MOON

WWW.APEXEDITIONS.COM

Copyright © 2026 by Apex Editions, Mendota Heights, MN 55120. All rights reserved. No part of this book may be reproduced or utilized in any form or by any means without written permission from the publisher.

Apex is distributed by North Star Editions:
sales@northstareditions.com | 888-417-0195

Produced for Apex by Red Line Editorial.

Photographs ©: Jay LaPrete/AP Images, cover, 1; Shutterstock Images, 4–5, 50–51, 52–53, 58–59; Gaelen Morse/Getty Images Sport/Getty Images, 6–7; Wikimedia Commons, 8–9; Underwood Archives/Archive Photos/Getty Images, 10–11; Bettmann/Getty Images, 12–13, 19, 22–23, 24–25, 26–27; Paul Shane/AP Images, 14–15; Gene Herrick/AP Images, 16–17; AP Images, 20–21, 29, 57; Jonathan Daniel/Allsport/Getty Images Sport/Getty Images, 30–31; Paul Sakuma/AP Images, 32–33; Patrick Green/Icon Sportswire/AP Images, 34–35; Kevin C. Cox/Getty Images Sport/Getty Images, 36–37; Al Messerschmidt/AP Images, 39; Jonathan Daniel/Getty Images Sport/Getty Images, 40–41; Ted S. Warren/AP Images, 42–43; Gregory Shamus/Getty Images Sport/Getty Images, 44–45; Don Juan Moore/Getty Images Sport/Getty Images, 46–47; Jamie Sabau/Getty Images Sport/Getty Images, 48–49; Aaron J. Thornton/Getty Images Sport/Getty Images, 54–55

Library of Congress Control Number: 2025930932

ISBN
979-8-89250-714-1 (hardcover)
979-8-89250-766-0 (paperback)
979-8-89250-749-3 (ebook pdf)
979-8-89250-732-5 (hosted ebook)

Printed in the United States of America
Mankato, MN
082025

NOTE TO PARENTS AND EDUCATORS

Apex books are designed to build literacy skills in striving readers. Exciting, high-interest content attracts and holds readers' attention. The text is carefully leveled to allow students to achieve success quickly.

TABLE OF CONTENTS

CHAPTER 1
O-H-I-O! 4

CHAPTER 2
EARLY HISTORY 8

PLAYER SPOTLIGHT
BILL WILLIS 18

CHAPTER 3
LEGENDS 20

PLAYER SPOTLIGHT
ARCHIE GRIFFIN 28

CHAPTER 4
RECENT HISTORY 30

PLAYER SPOTLIGHT
EDDIE GEORGE 38

CHAPTER 5
MODERN STARS 40

CHAPTER 6
TEAM TRIVIA 48

TEAM RECORDS • 56
TIMELINE • 58
COMPREHENSION QUESTIONS • 60
GLOSSARY • 62
TO LEARN MORE • 63
ABOUT THE AUTHOR • 63
INDEX • 64

CHAPTER 1
O-H-I-O!

More than 100,000 Ohio State fans are on their feet. One section yells "O." Another calls out "H." Then comes "I." The last section yells "O." The chant is famous across college football. The lights are shining. Everyone is cheering. It's game time at Ohio Stadium.

Ohio State fans dress in scarlet and gray to support their team.

Wide receiver Marvin Harrison Jr. hauls in a touchdown catch during a 2022 game against Arkansas State.

A Buckeyes wide receiver races toward the end zone. The quarterback launches a pass. Two defenders try to stop it. But the receiver grabs the ball. It's a touchdown! The Buckeyes are on their way to another win.

BLOCK O

A Buckeyes cheerleader created Block O in 1938. This student group still leads cheers at Ohio Stadium. The students often use cards to create pictures or words.

CHAPTER 2
EARLY HISTORY

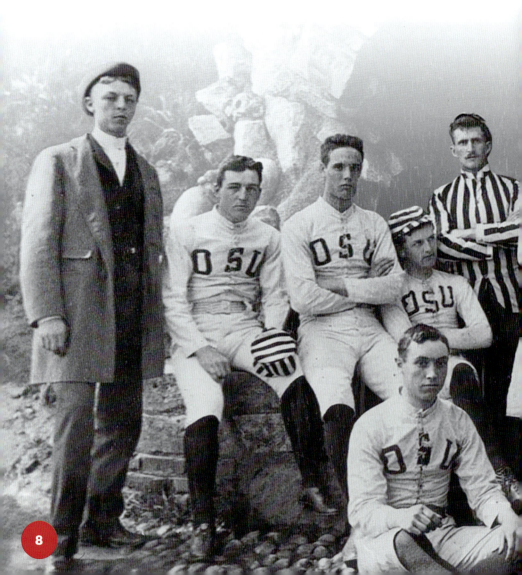

The Ohio State University dates back to 1870. The school's football team started 20 years later. Ohio State won its first game. The 20–14 victory came against Ohio Wesleyan. Ohio State first played Michigan in 1897. That was the start of one of football's greatest rivalries.

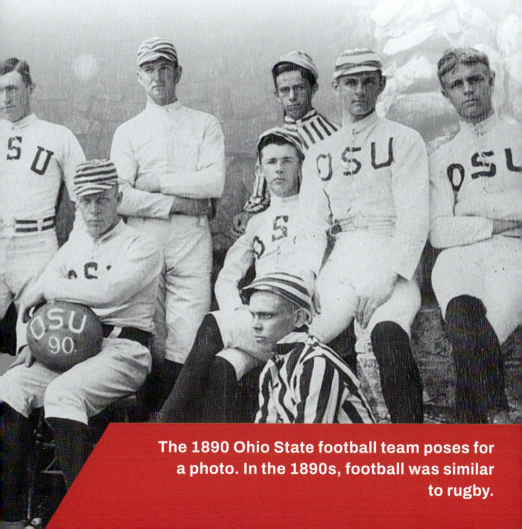

The 1890 Ohio State football team poses for a photo. In the 1890s, football was similar to rugby.

Ohio State players try to defend a pass during a 1927 game against Princeton.

In 1916, Ohio State won the conference title for the first time. Today, that conference is known as the Big Ten.

Francis Schmidt took over as head coach in 1934. He brought a flashy new style of play. The press called it "Razzle-Dazzle." Schmidt's teams won 39 games in seven seasons.

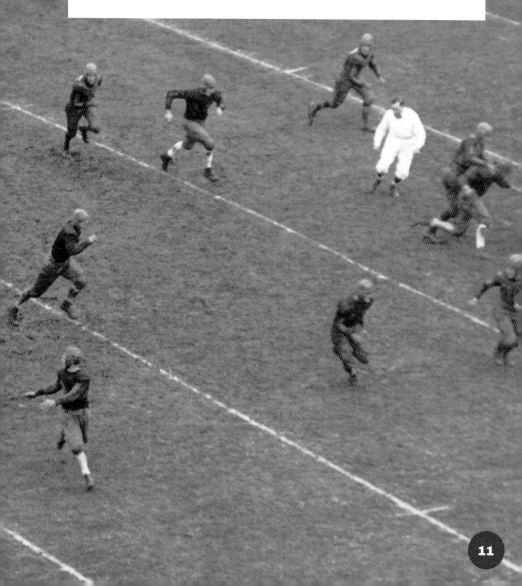

In 1941, Paul Brown took over as head coach. His 1942 team piled up points all season long. Ohio State went 9–1. The school won its first national title. However, Brown left after just one more season.

OHIO LEGEND

In 1946, Paul Brown helped create the Cleveland Browns. He coached them to seven titles. Then he formed the Cincinnati Bengals in the 1960s. Brown treated coaching like a science. He helped change the game of football.

Paul Brown explains a play to his team during a practice in 1941.

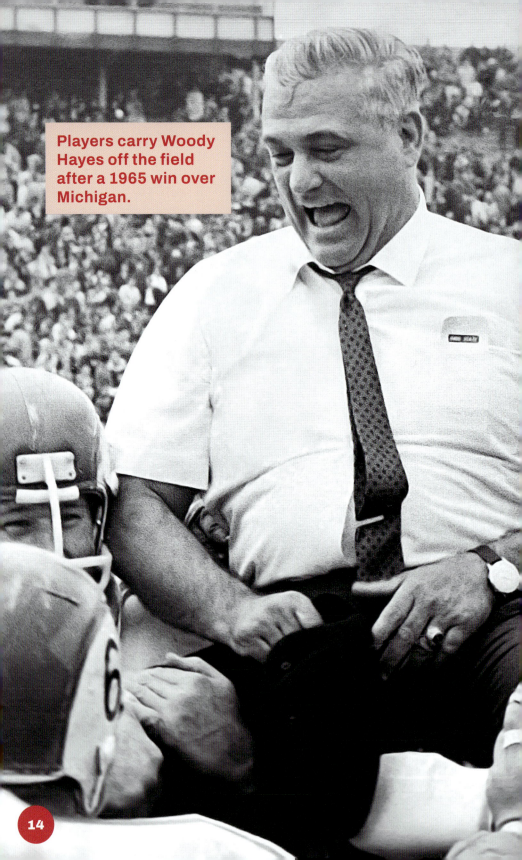

Players carry Woody Hayes off the field after a 1965 win over Michigan.

Head coach Woody Hayes led the Buckeyes from 1951 to 1978. He was known for being fiery. He hated to lose. And at Ohio State, he rarely did. Hayes focused on toughness. He called many running plays. Other teams had trouble stopping them.

BUCKEYES

Ohio became a state in 1803. By then, locals were calling one another "buckeyes." The buckeye is a type of tree. It's common in Ohio. So, it became a nickname for Ohio State's sports teams. The school made the name official in 1950.

Many fans consider Ohio State's 1968 team one of the best college football teams ever.

Ohio State won another national title in 1954. It was the first of five in Hayes's era.

In a 1968 game, Ohio State crushed Michigan. Late the fourth quarter, the Buckeyes scored a touchdown. It gave them a 50–14 lead. Hayes went for a two-point conversion. A reporter asked him why he did it. Hayes supposedly said, "because I couldn't go for three."

THE 10-YEAR WAR

Michigan became a power under coach Bo Schembechler. He and Woody Hayes overlapped from 1969 to 1978. The "10-Year War" was a heated period in the rivalry.

17

PLAYER SPOTLIGHT

BILL WILLIS

Bill Willis played a key role in Ohio State's 1942 national title. He starred on both the offensive and defensive lines. Willis had amazing power. He also had a sprinter's speed. He cleared away defenders with big blocks. And he dragged down ball carriers with his hard tackling.

Willis played his last college season in 1944. At the time, pro teams refused to sign Black players. But in 1946, that changed. Willis became one of four Black players to go pro.

BILL WILLIS WAS VOTED INTO THE COLLEGE FOOTBALL HALL OF FAME IN 1971.

CHAPTER 3

LEGENDS

Halfback Chic Harley set the standard at Ohio State. In the late 1910s, he became a three-time All-American. In the 1930s, halfback Lew Hinchman matched him. So did ends Wesley Fesler and Merle Wendt.

Merle Wendt served as the captain of Ohio State's 1936 team.

Halfback Les Horvath helped his team win a national title in 1942. In 1944, he started playing quarterback, too. Horvath was great at both positions. He won the Heisman Trophy. That award is given to the country's best college football player. In 1950, Vic Janowicz became Ohio State's second Heisman winner. He played halfback and defensive back.

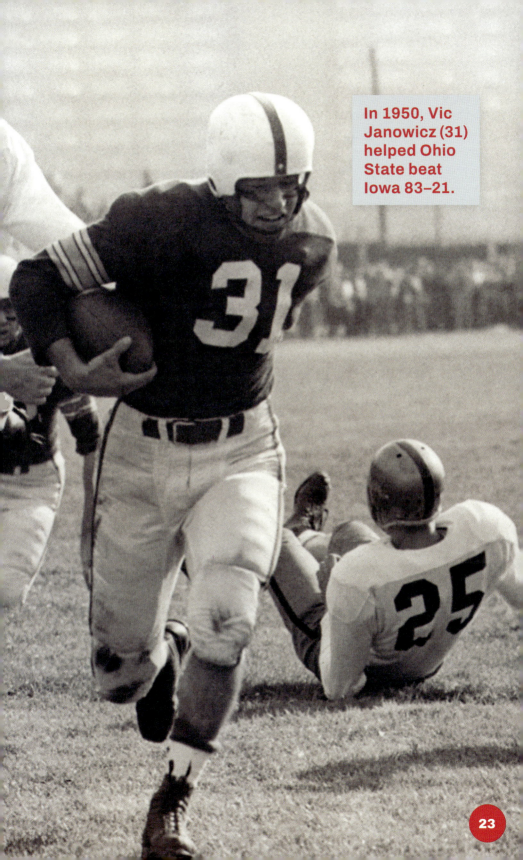

In 1950, Vic Janowicz (31) helped Ohio State beat Iowa 83–21.

Howard Cassady gained 2,982 total yards in his four years with the Buckeyes.

Ohio State won another national title in 1954. Halfback Howard Cassady was a big reason why.

The Buckeyes won national titles in 1957 and 1961. And they weren't done yet. In 1968 and 1970, defensive back Jack Tatum helped them win two more. Running back Archie Griffin kept the Buckeyes strong in the 1970s.

HOLD THE LINE

The Outland Trophy is given to the best interior lineman each year. Ohio State's Jim Parker won it in 1956. Jim Stillwagon and John Hicks both won it in the early 1970s.

The Buckeyes continued to shine in the 1980s. Running back Keith Byars powered the offense. In 1984, he led the nation with 1,655 rushing yards. Wide receiver Cris Carter caught just about everything that came his way. He scored 27 touchdowns as a Buckeye. And linebacker Chris Spielman was a tackling machine.

RECORD SETTER

Linebacker Tom Cousineau dominated in the late 1970s. He left Ohio State with several tackling records. In 1978, he recorded 211 tackles. Going into 2025, that remained a school record.

Cris Carter (2) makes an amazing catch during the 1987 Cotton Bowl.

PLAYER SPOTLIGHT

ARCHIE GRIFFIN

Archie Griffin was short for a tailback. He wasn't the fastest player either. But when he took a handoff, none of that mattered. Griffin was one of the best who ever played the game. He sliced through defenses. Defenders thought they were in position to stop him. Then he slipped past them.

Griffin topped 1,300 rushing yards three years in a row. He won the Heisman Trophy in both 1974 and 1975. As of 2025, Griffin was still the only two-time winner.

> **ARCHIE GRIFFIN RAN FOR 5,177 YARDS IN HIS FOUR YEARS AT OHIO STATE.**

CHAPTER 4
RECENT HISTORY

Woody Hayes left after the 1978 season. But the Buckeyes remained great. Head coaches Earle Bruce and John Cooper both won lots of games. Cooper's 1996 team finished second in the nation. His 1998 team also finished second.

In the 1998 season, the Buckeyes beat Texas A&M 24–14 in the Sugar Bowl.

Jim Tressel lifts the trophy after leading the Buckeyes to a national title in the 2002 season.

Ohio State turned to coach Jim Tressel in 2001. He put together a talented team. In 2002, the Buckeyes went undefeated. They reached the national title game. Few expected them to beat the Miami Hurricanes. But the Buckeyes won 31–24 in double overtime. The victory gave Ohio State its seventh national title.

The Buckeyes returned to the national title game in 2006 and 2007. However, Ohio State lost both times. In 2014, a new four-team playoff started. Ohio State made it as the fourth team. First, they beat top-ranked Alabama. Then they beat Oregon. The season ended with another national title.

GAME OF THE CENTURY

In 2006, Ohio State and Michigan met as the nation's two best teams. A spot in the national title game was on the line. The Buckeyes pulled off the win. They treated their home fans to a 42–39 victory.

Quarterback Cardale Jones runs for a touchdown during the national title game of the 2014 season.

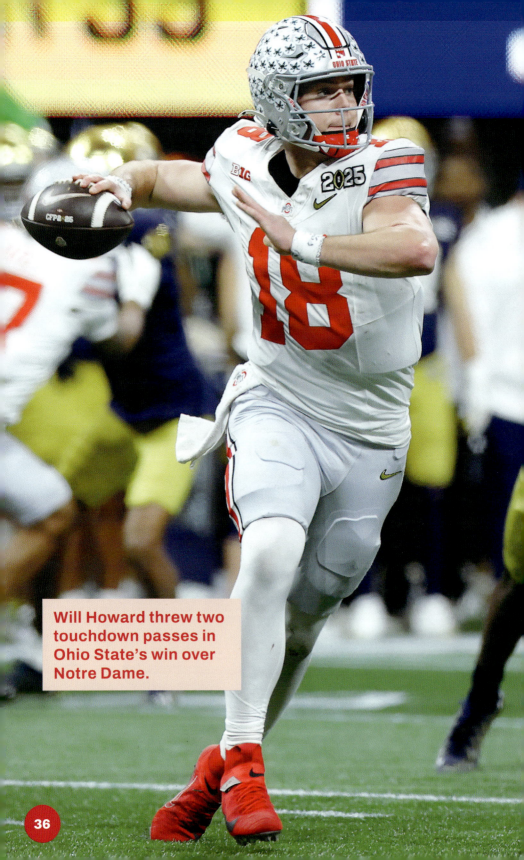

Will Howard threw two touchdown passes in Ohio State's win over Notre Dame.

Head coach Urban Meyer led Ohio State from 2012 to 2018. Under Meyer, the team never lost more than two games in a season. Ohio State's winning ways continued under Ryan Day. In 2024, he led the Buckeyes to another national title. Ohio State beat Notre Dame 34–23 in the championship game.

STREAKING

From 2001 to 2019, the Buckeyes went 17–2 against Michigan. That included a seven-game winning streak. Then Michigan won one. But Ohio State won the next eight. However, things changed in the early 2020s. The Buckeyes dropped their fourth in a row against Michigan in 2024.

PLAYER SPOTLIGHT

EDDIE GEORGE

As a kid, Eddie George dreamed of winning the Heisman Trophy. He even practiced his victory speech in front of the mirror. He got his chance at Ohio State.

George had great size for a running back. He was also fast. By his senior year in 1995, George was nearly unstoppable. He powered his way to 1,826 rushing yards. He also scored 24 touchdowns. George ended the season by winning the Heisman Trophy. His dream had come true.

EDDIE GEORGE RECORDED MORE THAN 4,000 TOTAL YARDS AS A BUCKEYE.

CHAPTER 5
MODERN STARS

Pass rushers couldn't do much against Orlando Pace. The huge offensive tackle flattened defenders with his blocks. That's how he earned the nickname "Pancake Man." In 1994 and 1995, Pace helped clear the way for Eddie George.

In his last two years with Ohio State, Orlando Pace (75) didn't allow a single sack.

Maurice Clarett scores the winning touchdown in the national title game of the 2002 season.

Few Buckeyes tackled quite like Mike Doss. The safety helped Ohio State win a national title in 2002. Cornerback Chris Gamble also played a big role on defense that season.

On offense, a freshman became the team's star. Running back Maurice Clarett racked up 1,341 total yards. He also scored 18 touchdowns. His last score was in double overtime of the national title game.

Troy Smith threw for 5,720 yards and 54 touchdowns in three seasons.

Some experts thought Troy Smith would play wide receiver in college. Ohio State stuck with him at quarterback. The decision paid off in 2006. Smith was nearly perfect as a passer. He led the Buckeyes back to the national title game. And he easily won the Heisman Trophy.

STUD LINEBACKERS

A. J. Hawk was one of Ohio State's best linebackers ever. He left in 2005. That year, fellow linebacker James Laurinaitis was just getting started. Laurinaitis became the school's eighth three-time All-American.

Ezekiel Elliott leaves Oregon defenders in the dust during the national title game of the 2014 season.

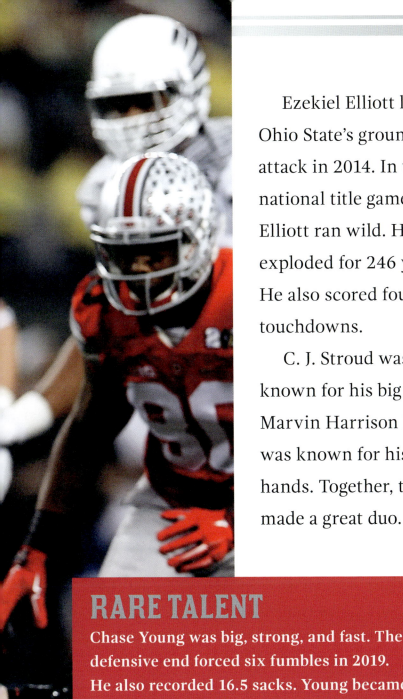

Ezekiel Elliott led Ohio State's ground attack in 2014. In the national title game, Elliott ran wild. He exploded for 246 yards. He also scored four touchdowns.

C. J. Stroud was known for his big arm. Marvin Harrison Jr. was known for his sure hands. Together, they made a great duo.

RARE TALENT

Chase Young was big, strong, and fast. The defensive end forced six fumbles in 2019. He also recorded 16.5 sacks. Young became a Heisman Trophy finalist. That's rare for a defensive player.

CHAPTER 6
TEAM TRIVIA

Fans love watching the Ohio State Marching Band. The band is known for a drill called Script Ohio. Band members start by forming an "O" on the field. Soon, they line up to spell "Ohio." Then a tuba player dots the "i."

A marching tuba is called a sousaphone. It wraps around the player's body.

Ohio Stadium's horseshoe shape is still visible even though new stands have been added.

Ohio Stadium seats more than 102,000 fans. Only a few stadiums in the world are bigger. The stadium opened in 1922. At first, it had stands on three sides. So, it looked like a big horseshoe. More stands were added in the early 2000s. Now, the seating goes all the way around the field. However, fans still call the stadium "The Horseshoe."

VICTORY BELL

The Victory Bell sits in a tower at Ohio Stadium. It rings after every Ohio State home win. The giant bell weights 2,420 pounds (1,100 kg). It can be heard 5 miles (8 km) away.

Scarlet and gray have been Ohio State's official school colors since 1878.

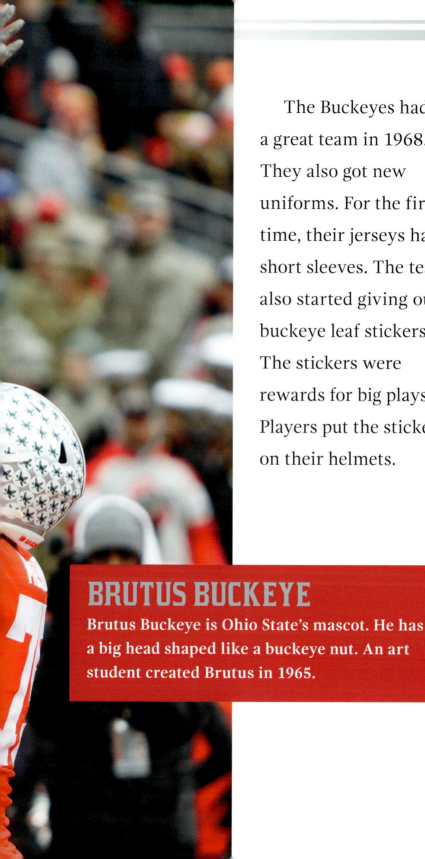

The Buckeyes had a great team in 1968. They also got new uniforms. For the first time, their jerseys had short sleeves. The team also started giving out buckeye leaf stickers. The stickers were rewards for big plays. Players put the stickers on their helmets.

BRUTUS BUCKEYE

Brutus Buckeye is Ohio State's mascot. He has a big head shaped like a buckeye nut. An art student created Brutus in 1965.

Many people in Ohio refer to Michigan as "the school up north."

The Buckeyes have several rivals. Ohio State and Illinois play for the Illibuck trophy. Ohio State also has a rivalry with Penn State. But nothing compares to "The Game." That's what fans call the annual meeting with Michigan. The teams have played each other more than 120 times.

GOLD CHARM

Michigan shut out the Buckeyes three times in the early 1930s. In 1934, Ohio State coach Francis Schmidt didn't want his team to worry. So, he told his players that the Wolverines put on their pants one leg at a time, just like everyone else. Ohio State won. Today, every Buckeyes player gets a little gold charm when Ohio State beats Michigan. The charm is a pair of football pants.

TEAM RECORDS

All-Time Passing Yards: 9,434
J. T. Barrett (2014–17)

All-Time Rushing Yards: 5,589
Archie Griffin (1972–75)

All-Time Receiving Yards: 2,898
Michael Jenkins (2000–03)

All-Time Scoring: 356
Mike Nugent (2001–04)

All-Time Interceptions: 22
Mike Sensibaugh (1968–70)

All-Time Sacks: 36
Mike Vrabel (1993–96)

All-Time Tackles: 572
Marcus Marek (1979–82)

All-Time Coaching Wins: 205
Woody Hayes (1951–78)

Heisman Trophy Winners: 7
Les Horvath (1944), Vic Janowicz (1950), Howard Cassady (1955), Archie Griffin (1974, 1975), Eddie George (1995), Troy Smith (2006)

National Championships: 9
1942, 1954†, 1957†, 1961†, 1968, 1970†, 2002, 2014, 2024

† Season in which more than one school claims the national title.

All statistics are accurate through 2024.

TIMELINE

1890 | **1921** | **1942** | **1944** | **1951**

1890 — On May 3, Ohio State plays its first football game, beating Ohio Wesleyan 20–14.

1921 — On January 1, Ohio State plays in its first bowl game but falls to Cal 28–0 in the Rose Bowl.

1942 — Ohio State finishes the season 9–1 and is named national champion for the first time.

1944 — Halfback Les Horvath becomes the first Ohio State player to win the Heisman Trophy.

1951 — Woody Hayes takes over as Ohio State's coach. He leads the team for the next 28 seasons.

58

1955 — On January 1, Ohio State beats Cal in the Rose Bowl and earns another national title.

1968 — Ohio State goes for a late two-point conversion in a 50–14 win over Michigan. The Buckeyes go on to earn another national title.

1975 — Ohio State running back Archie Griffin becomes the first player to win the Heisman Trophy twice.

2003 — On January 3, the Buckeyes stun the Miami Hurricanes in double overtime to win the national title.

2025 — Ohio State beats Notre Dame on January 20 to claim the ninth national title in school history.

COMPREHENSION QUESTIONS

Write your answers on a separate piece of paper.

1. Write a paragraph that explains the main ideas of Chapter 4.

2. Who do you think was the greatest coach in Buckeyes history? Why?

3. Who was the first Ohio State player to win the Heisman Trophy?
    - A. Archie Griffin
    - B. Les Horvath
    - C. Vic Janowicz

4. Why is Ohio Stadium nicknamed "The Horseshoe"?
    - A. The stadium hosted many horse races in the early 1900s.
    - B. The stadium was originally shaped like a horseshoe.
    - C. The team buried a lucky horseshoe under one of the end zones.

5. What does **era** mean in this book?

*Ohio State won another national title in 1954. It was the first of five in Hayes's **era**.*

- A. a period in time
- B. a winning season
- C. a successful coach

6. What does **dominated** mean in this book?

*Linebacker Tom Cousineau **dominated** in the late 1970s. He left Ohio State with several tackling records.*

- A. won fewer games than usual
- B. ran slower than teammates
- C. played better than opponents

Answer key on page 64.

GLOSSARY

All-American
A player named as one of the best in the country in his or her sport.

conference
A group of teams that make up part of a sports league.

freshman
A student in his or her first year of college.

mascot
A figure that is the symbol of a sports team.

overtime
An extra period that happens if two teams are tied at the end of the fourth quarter.

playoff
A set of games played after the regular season to decide which team is the champion.

rivalries
Ongoing competitions that bring out strong emotion from fans and players.

sacks
Plays that happen when a defender tackles the quarterback before he can throw the ball.

two-point conversion
A play that a team can try after scoring a touchdown. To score the extra two points, a team must get the ball into the end zone from the 3-yard line.

TO LEARN MORE

BOOKS

Ellenport, Craig. *Ohio State Buckeyes*. The Child's World, 2022.

Hewson, Anthony K. *C. J. Stroud: Football Superstar*. Press Box Books, 2025.

Hunter, Tony. *Ohio State Buckeyes*. Abdo Publishing, 2021.

ONLINE RESOURCES

Visit **www.apexeditions.com** to find links and resources related to this title.

ABOUT THE AUTHOR

Derek Moon is an author and avid Stratego player who lives in Watertown, Massachusetts, with his wife and daughter.

INDEX

Brown, Paul, 12
Bruce, Earle, 30
Byars, Keith, 26

Carter, Cris, 26
Cassady, Howard, 25
Clarett, Maurice, 43
Cooper, John, 30
Cousineau, Tom, 26

Day, Ryan, 37
Doss, Mike, 43

Elliot, Ezekiel, 47

Fesler, Wesley, 20

Gamble, Chris, 43
George, Eddie, 38, 40
Griffin, Archie, 25, 28

Harley, Chic, 20
Harrison, Marvin, Jr., 47
Hawk, A. J., 45
Hayes, Woody, 15, 17, 30
Hicks, John, 25

Hinchman, Lew, 20
Horvath, Les, 22

Janowicz, Vic, 22

Laurinaitis, James, 45

Meyer, Urban, 37

Ohio Stadium, 5, 7, 51

Pace, Orlando, 40
Parker, Jim, 26

Schmidt, Francis, 11, 55
Smith, Troy, 45
Spielman, Chris, 26
Stroud, C. J., 47

Tatum, Jack, 25
Tressel, Jim, 33

Wendt, Merle, 20
Willis, Bill, 18

Young, Chase, 47

ANSWER KEY:
1. Answers will vary; 2. Answers will vary; 3. B; 4. B; 5. A; 6. C